D1286674

# Woodland Wildlife

# North American Black Bears

by G. G. Lake

CAPSTONE PRESS
a capstone imprint

Pebble®
Plus

Pebble Plus is published by Capstone Press,
1710 Roe Crest Drive, North Mankato, Minnesota 56003
www.mycapstone.com

**Library of Congress Cataloging-in-Publication Data**
Names: Lake, G. G., author.
Title: North American Black bears / by G. G. Lake.
Description: North Mankato, Minnesota : Capstone Press, [2017] | Series:
    Pebble plus. Woodland wildlife | Audience: Ages 4–8 | Audience: K to
    grade 3 | Includes bibliographical references and index.
Identifiers: LCCN 2016001920| ISBN 9781515708148 (library binding) | ISBN
    9781515708216 (pbk.) | ISBN 9781515708278 (ebook (pdf))
Subjects:  LCSH: Black bear—Juvenile literature.
Classification: LCC QL737.C27 L3275 2017 | DDC 599.78/5—dc23
LC record available at http://lccn.loc.gov/2016001920

**Editorial Credits**
Gena Chester, editor; Juliette Peters, designer;
Wanda Winch, media researcher; Steve Walker, production specialist

**Photo Credits**
Corbis: Design Pics/Michael DeYoung, 17; iStockphoto: Dieter Meyri, 19; Shutterstock:
alicedaniel, illustrated forest items, Anna Subbotina, 22–23, AR Pictures, tree bark
design, Critterbiz, cover, 5, 13, elina, 24, Ian Maton, 9, jadimages, 21, mythja, 1, Stawek,
11 (map), Sunny Forest, 3; Thinkstock: Bjorn Bakstad, 11 (top), Capturing_Essence, 7,
Frank Hildebrand, 15; Visuals Unlimited, Tom Ulrich, 12

## Note to Parents and Teachers

The Woodland Wildlife set supports national curriculum standards for science related
to life science. This book describes and illustrates North American black bears. The
images support early readers in understanding the text. The repetition of words and
phrases helps early readers learn new words. This book also introduces early readers
to subject-specific vocabulary words, which are defined in the Glossary section. Early
readers may need assistance to read some words and to use the Table of Contents,
Glossary, Read More, Internet Sites, Critical Thinking Using the Common Core,
and Index sections of the book.

Printed and bound in
China PO007726LEOF16

# Table of Contents

# Clawed Climbers

A big black animal climbs

up a tree. His curved claws

and big paws help him climb fast.

He's a North American black bear!

All black bears have strong bodies. Their legs are short but powerful. Most adult black bears weigh at least 200 pounds (91 kilograms).

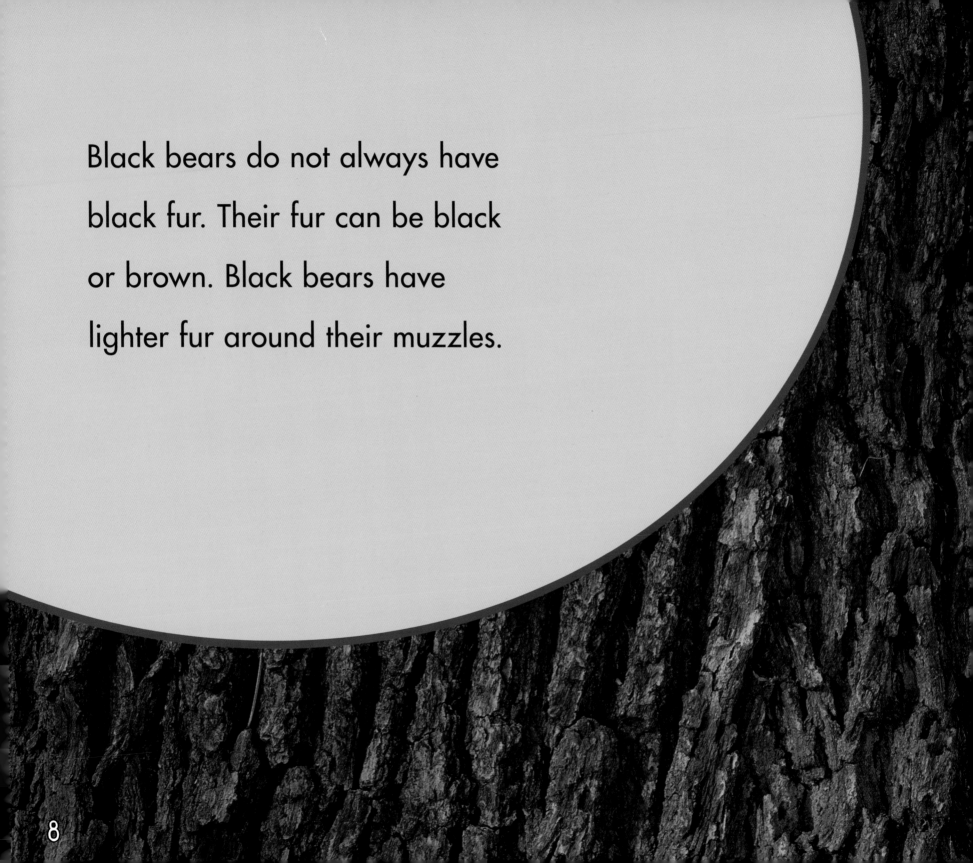

Black bears do not always have black fur. Their fur can be black or brown. Black bears have lighter fur around their muzzles.

muzzle

# Forest Homes

Black bears are found
throughout North America.
They live in the woods and
near water.

# North American Black Bear Range Map

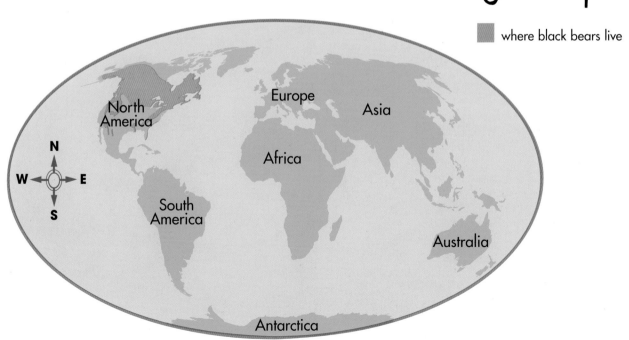

Europe

Asia

North
America

Africa

N

W E

S

South
America

Australia

Antarctica

Black bears live in homes called dens. A den can be found in many places. It can be in a cave, a hollow log, or dug into the ground.

# Finding Food

Black bears are not picky eaters. They eat berries, bugs, and fish. Black bears sniff with their noses to find food.

Black bears can smell food at
campsites. Campers keep their
food away from bears.
Campers hide their food and
pick up their trash.

# Life Cycle

A mother black bear gives birth to one to five cubs at a time. Her babies are born covered in fur. The cubs are born blind.

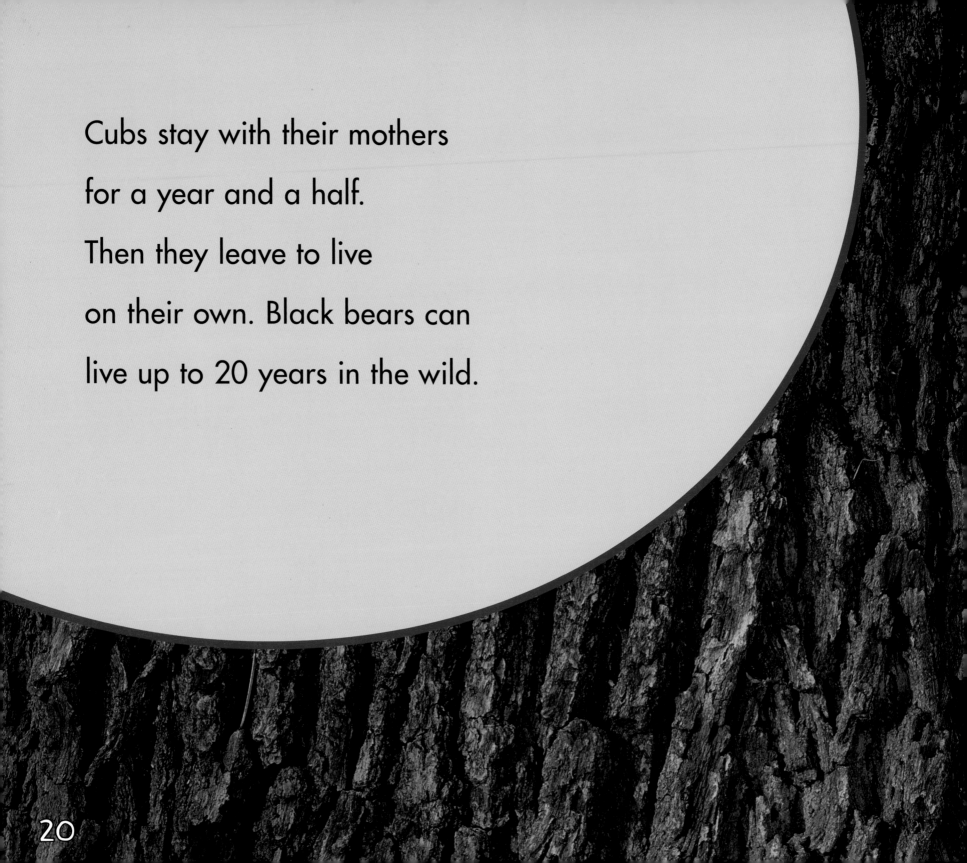

Cubs stay with their mothers
for a year and a half.
Then they leave to live
on their own. Black bears can
live up to 20 years in the wild.

# Glossary

**blind**—unable to see or having very limited sight

**cub**—a young bear

**den**—a place where a wild animal may live; a den may be a hole in the ground or a trunk of a tree

**fur**—thick hair that covers an animal

**hollow**—empty on the inside

**muzzle**—an animal's nose, mouth, and jaw

**woods**—a large area covered with trees and plants; forests are sometimes called woods

# Read More

**Borgert-Spaniol, Megan.** *Black Bears.* North American Animals. Minneapolis: Bellwether Media, 2015.

**Kolpin, Molly.** *American Black Bears.* Bears. Mankato, Minn.: Capstone Press, 2012.

**Magby, Meryl.** *Black Bears.* American Animals. New York: PowerKids Press, 2014.

# Internet Sites

FactHound offers a safe, fun way to find Internet sites related to this book. All of the sites on FactHound have been researched by our staff.

Here's all you do:

Visit *www.facthound.com*

Type in this code: 9781515708148

Check out projects, games and lots more at
**www.capstonekids.com**

# Critical Thinking
## Using the Common Core

1. What helps black bears climb trees? (Key Ideas and Details)

2. What is a den? (Craft and Structure)

3. How long do cubs stay with their mothers? (Key Ideas and Details)

# Index

**28** DAY LOAN
**Hewlett-Woodmere Public Library**
**Hewlett, New York 11557**

**Business Phone 516-374-1967**
**Recorded Announcements 516-374-1667**
**Website www.hwpl.org**